Lorena Lohr

DESERT NUDES

SOHO REVUE

Introduction

CASSIE BEADLE

Desert Nudes is an ongoing series of oil on panel paintings by Lorena Lohr, created over a ten year period, culminating in her first collected publication. Lohr is primarily known as a photographer, and the works thus represent an extension of her self-taught artistic practice.

The series is fundamentally influenced by Lohr's independent travels across the USA by train and Greyhound bus. Lohr's many long trips across the American Southwest spurred her to create a body of work that harmonises the desert landscape with the female form. Painted at a small scale in a muted, dusky palette and in delicate verisimilitude, the works recall the intimacy of Northern Renaissance devotional paintings. For Lohr, these works are commemorative of the desert, exploring the idea that this landscape, a barren expanse, is also rich with certain forms of life. Similarly, the desert is a fertile artistic landscape for Lohr, and assumes the leading role within and across her photographic and painting practice.

Arguably, Lohr's desire to paint directly ties in with her photographic work – her handprints are often painstakingly finished with dyes and by hand. At the same time, Lohr's still life photographic works, particularly those of buildings and signage, evoke painting qualities in texture, colour, surface and composition. Much like her photographs, Lohr's Desert Nudes are born from an intuitive creative process and can be read as semi-diaristic. Forms and lines pattern out from Lohr's memories of places visited and rooms inhabited while travelling along the border of Mexico and the Southwestern desert towns of North America.

A sense of solitude permeates the works, perhaps reflective of the conditions and experiences which informed their creation. To teach herself to paint, Lohr transformed a closet in her apartment into a makeshift studio, where she spent sleepless nights perfecting her painterly language. For Lohr, the desert and the female form are intrinsically linked. Lohr's female subjects appear suspended in time, mid gesture; luxuriating in their surroundings, fluctuating between moments of longing or hope. Moving between both interior and exterior, both the wood-panelled rooms and desert backdrops become pathetic fallacy to the subject's inner world: the nudes and figures bend and blend with the spaces in which they are situated.

The characters Lohr paints are, for her, emblematic of escapism, imbued with the promise of and need for freedom. Her rendering of female archetypes, meanwhile, reinforces them as universal allegories of desire. She subtly pays homage to the artistic language found in Mannerist painting of the 1530s, works depicting landscapes populated with classical figures, with an emphasis on natural beauty. By contrast, Lohr's Desert Nudes also alight on the entrenched machismo associated with the American West. Lohr reclaims the desert from archetypes of masculinity, replacing the classic characterisations of outlaw and cowboy with her imagined, female counterparts, who are elevated to the near-mythological – deities in their own fantasy realm.

Creating works in the traditional technique of oil on panel, Lohr studied and collected reproductions of Northern Renaissance paintings from libraries and second hand bookstores. As such, the works in Desert Nudes parody defining tropes from this era. The most innovative feature of landscape painting in the 1400s and 1500s was the conception of landscape as a vast terrain with deeply receding space. Artists began to depict the distant horizon and capture the palpable atmosphere between the viewer's vantage point and the horizon. Flemish artists painted portraits often featuring desert landscapes evocative of biblical stories. The background was often seen through windows, a tool to bring the spiritual world closer to the real – to make attainable the unattainable. Similarly, Madonna figures were depicted in the domestic environment, in attempts to bring the holy figure into familiar spaces, as a way to enhance the experience of private worship for the patron.

Lohr observes that while Columbus arrived in the Americas in the late 15th century, around the time the Northern Renaissance was at its peak, the American desert largely remained unexplored by Europeans until centuries later. As such, Lohr brings the credence and aesthetics of the Northern Renaissance to the 'New Frontier' – a vast, wild and poetic landscape still unexploited in the time of the Northern Renaissance artists. In Lohr's works, nude figures could be understood as desert mirages, mythological goddesses or holy apparitions. The Madonna in a domestic interior is supplanted by a blonde in blue jeans, framed by the wood panelling of an American bar. The devotional quality of these works is enhanced by their encasement in reliquary-like frames constructed from raw silk. In this way, Lohr offers her very own brand of private worship – that of the spiritually enduring and mystical realm of the desert.

PAINTINGS
2014 - 2024

Blonde Desert Nude

Desert Springs

Arizona Nude

Two Girls in Jeans

Untitled 1

Desert Nude

Girl in Texas

Girl in Bar Room

Bar Room Interior with Pool Cues

Girl on Bed at Night

Bar Room Blonde

Girl in Motel Room

Desert Nude with Drink

Desert Nude at Dusk

Girl and Adobe House

Desert Nude and Waterfall

Desert Nude at Night II

Desert Nude on Rocks

Desert Nude at Dawn

Bar Room Nude

Nude and Motel Room Doors

Girl in Blue Room at Night

Girl in Yuma

LIST OF WORKS

Blonde Desert Nude, 2015 - 2018	5 x 8 Inches
Desert Springs, 2014 - 2018	7¾ x 11¼ Inches
Arizona Nude, 2014 - 2016	5 x 8 Inches
Two Girls in Jeans, 2015 - 2020	8 x 10 Inches
Untitled 1, 2016 - 2019	8 x 11¾ Inches
Desert Nude, 2014 - 2018	11 x 14 Inches
Girl in Texas, 2020 - 2022	8 x 9⅝ Inches
Girl in Bar Room, 2020 - 2022	8¼ x 11 Inches
Bar Room Interior with Pool Cues, 2022 - 2023	4⅜ x 6 Inches
Girl on Bed at Night, 2022 - 2023	8 x 10 Inches
Bar Room Blonde, 2020 - 2023	8 x 11 Inches
Girl in Motel Room, 2020 - 2023	5⅛ x 7½ Inches

Desert Nude with Drink, 2020 - 2023	.. 5 x 7 Inches
Desert Nude at Dusk, 2020 - 2023	.. 6½ x 9¼ Inches
Girl and Adobe House, 2017 - 2022	.. 5 x 7 Inches
Desert Nude and Waterfall, 2021 - 2023	.. 6 x 8⅝ Inches
Desert Nude at Night II, 2023	.. 6¼ x 10¼ Inches
Desert Nude on Rocks, 2022 - 2024	.. 8¾ x 12 Inches
Desert Nude at Dawn, 2022 - 2024	.. 9⅛ x 11⅞ Inches
Bar Room Nude, 2023 - 2024	.. 4⅜ x 5¾ Inches
Nude and Motel Room Doors, 2023 - 2024	.. 8¼ x 11¾ Inches
Girl in Blue Room at Night, 2023 - 2024	.. 5⅝ x 6¼ Inches
Girl in Yuma, 2023 - 2024	.. 8⅛ x 12 Inches
Back Cover - Sunset Nude, 2024	.. 2⅛ Inch diameter

All paintings oil on panel

BURNING **L**OVE AND **H**OT **O**IL

I was wiping down the long wood bar – whiskey, syrup and fizz. The evening lulled on, only the regulars sat round, gazing down into amber beer with strands of oiled hair falling over their foreheads. Waylon S. Franchise arranged toothpicks into a Model Ford, Henry lit a match. Outside the light was dusky, birds rested on a telephone pole, and shadows passed briefly over the smoked-glass window. The radio spoke hushed, then soared up to a swirled vocal, crooning of paradise gardens, hilltop romance and the hours before dawn.

In the corner of the room, I dusted a jar. I fixed up the pool balls on the blue felt table, placed the cue upright. A Western scene played out in a faded wall mural behind the bar booths – tobacco-stained buffalo and stagecoaches. Then the door frame creaked, boot heels dragging on wood. I turned around, eyeing up tight muscle and blue jean – precision-fit over his strong hips. A white t-shirt contrasted sun-browned arms and hands that stroked the dry air.

Gazing on this man and his burden, a teardrop fell from my right eye and pooled out on the surface of a red naugahyde barstool. I fainted to the slatted floor and came to suspended in his grip. His warmth lit me, glowing hot. The daytime men faded and were cut out of vision by spotlight as he bore me lightly down atop the pool table, fingers resting a moment on my hips. His veined hand cast shadows across my face, and before long he pulled a folded chair from the barside wall. He placed me tabletop, my ass over the edge, slinging toothpicks and red straws to the ground.

I heard the pull of leather and metal as his stud belt slacked down, a crystal cobra bouncing on his thigh. A hand crept up my back, and glancing sideways his face licked my shoulder, catching eyes in the mirror. Without word, he looked deeply through me and sent me up straight with that fire between his legs. I turned liquid, his motions jaunty and hostile and strong, pulling through me to the heart. His hair stuck to my lipstick and his voice spoke of lost nights. His fingers slid in my ear, blocking out all noise, then down to the inside of my thighs...

We were in a backlot in South Dakota, the freights passed slowly and floodlights burned the dust as we screwed on metal. The bar room lights of Music Row lit pools of rainwater, then turned to desert sun with buzzards flying overhead. We were in Tahiti, Casa Grande, Shreveport, Big Spring. We fucked through the Southern swamps, through Chicago in the 1930s, through Kentucky distilleries and Blue Avenue. We started on a round-the-world fuck, a fulfilled and everywhere fuck, passing Puerto Rican boys, hustlers, pretty girls in gingham and white bobby ankle socks, greasers, leather daddies, bums, the lost and lonesome – faces of longing and despair and tenderness flashed by as we hurled through time, Bruce's cock lighting me up like a battery in that tape player you listen to your first rock 'n' roll on, revving me up with all the secret knowledge of a sad boy burning in the night, making it all for himself, through the hard knocks and tough times. He turned me round and rode me like a hotrod, and over my shoulder I turned to see his strong brow and a crystal of sweat sliding down his Romanlike profile, like a plastic bead of rain on a dollar store synthetic rose.

As night came down we drove it on and on, gliding through the shady summer streets of his youth, under awnings with wind chimes and swaying flags and the powerlines connecting front room to front room. All kinds of stories were played out, reams and reams of concealed heartbreaks, yearnings and secret dreams, stories which in their sadness and truth would be unrecordable in their infinity. We passed tenement windows, water boilers on stoves and radios on top of refrigerators blasting lonely songs of desire. A kid picked up a fallen nickel from the ground on 110th Street, gazing at the high parkway overhead. In Cleveland, we fucked by amber-lit railyards, and a lone walker passing the factory gates at dawn. In Arizona, sagebrush stood in bunches on the edge of burnt asphalt. The tyres passed as we screwed in the bushes, my skin pricked raw by the thorns of creosote and mesquite. In Alaska, he burnt me with winter matches. In Louisiana, we screwed on the back of a nest of alligators – by the riverside, syrupy drunk on pink cherry wine.

In the casino towns, candy-apple-red flashes and blazed neon reflected in the whites of his eyes. Swinging lassoes, revolving restaurants, stilettos and motel signs spoke in lit-up motif. In New Jersey, we fucked in beachfront parking lots, the sand sticking in my armpits. In Minneapolis, we screwed there too. Upstairs in Chinatowns, old men sat throwing dice as we breathed heavily on tea-brown mattresses, ancient philosophies pouring over our bodies like drifting water. He whispered, 'You gotta make your own way baby,' as I stuck my fingers in his mouth, curls dripping wet around his dark eyes.

From mill town to mill town, over bayou and Cajun wood shacks, the highways pouring drifters every which ways, he tore me down. A forever screw, on and on, condemned for life. If we ever knew what we were really yearning for, we wouldn't be burning through the night. Bruce and I screwed to the end of time, mixing all our faith and doubt with everything that passed, taking in the darkness of every town, riding to the end.

Desert Nudes
Published by Soho Revue
14 Greek Street
London W1D 4DP
sohorevue.com

All images © Lorena Lohr
Printed 2024

Designed by Michael Nash Associates
in collaboration with Lorena Lohr

ISBN 978 1 3999 9740 9

All rights reserved by the authors and artists.
No part of this book may be reproduced, stored
in a retrieval system, or transmitted in any form
or by any means, electronic, mechanical,
photocopying, recording or otherwise, without
the written permission of the publisher.
Every reasonable effort has been made to
identify owners of copyright. Errors or
omissions will be corrected in subsequent editions.

Printed and bound in Latvia

Thanks to India Rose James at Soho Revue
Sasha Alcocer, Cassie Beadle, Louise Benson,
Rose Blake, Jarvis Cocker, Christine Connolly,
Claire Feasey, Rebecca Fourteau, Mary Frey,
Charlotte Grocutt, Elsa Hansen Oldham,
Marc Hare, Nell Hayes, Jacob at The Framing Room,
WW Jones, Bernice Knapfield, Lucy Kumara-Moore,
Zofi and Adam Lipton, Richard Lohr,
Georgia McGuinness, Jake McGuinness,
Anthony Michael, Harland Miller, Phoebe
Mitchell-Innes, Nadia Narain, Stephanie Nash,
OKS, Lucy Pratt, Manizeh Rimer, Marcy Robinson,
Miguel Santa Clara, Sophia Satchell-Baeza,
Marie-Louise Scio, Charlie Siddick, Kim Sion,
Heather Sommerfield, Mario Sorrenti, Brad Stainton,
Daniel Vildósola, Digby Warde-Aldam, Victoria Williams.